THIS PLACE THE GODS TOUCHED EARTH

THIS PLACE THE GODS TOUCHED EARTH

POETRY BY MONTANA'S POETS LAUREATE 2005–2025

EDITED BY KRYS HOLMES
AND ERIC HEIDLE

Published by
The Montana Arts Council
Montana Historical Society Press

2024

Printed in Canada.

Distributed by Farcountry Press, 2750 Broadwater Avenue, Helena, MT 59602
(800) 821-3874

ISBN 978-1-940527-05-5 (hardcover)

Library of Congress Cataloging-in-Publication Data available on request

Cover illustration by David Miles Lusk
Book design by Eric Heidle

For the people of this place called Montana

CONTENTS

PREFACE

Solstice at the cabin deep in the forest.
The full moon shines in the river, there are pale
green northern lights. A huge thunderstorm
comes slowly from the west. Lightning strikes
a nearby tamarack bursting into flame.
I go into the cabin feeling unworthy.
At dawn the tree is still smoldering
in this place the gods touched earth.

We beings of smoldering wonder. We sleepy creatures, struggling to open our eyes to the riven world where beauty and horror and despair and unspeakable mercies go on all around us—in the duff, beneath the snow, up in the tangle of branches, in our own ganglia. We Montanans, who inhabit a landscape of astounding beauty and restlessness and wind-addled spaciousness, and cannot, absolutely cannot put it all into words—we turn to those who seem oddly gifted with the capacity to flick, with a phrase or a line, a spark of truth to flame, like a ranch hand's thumbnail flicks a match. Those writers. Those poets.

Look alive, Montana's poets say, watch out. Wake up. This is not the time to forget who we are or where in this world some blessed force has set us. This is not the time to pretend not to know what we know: that the world is aflame with beauty, that all of life is as intertwined as the northern plains ecosystem, that we are all hoop dancing on the tiny crust of earth just inches (relatively) from the magma, and however we spend our four thousand weeks of life we will leave nothing behind but dust and love, the ratio of which is our legacy to the living.

I believe Montana is the place the gods touched earth. I can't help but believe it. Part of the way the divine touches us is through the work of these eleven poets laureate (the word means honored one). Each laureate serves for two years, crisscrossing the state giving readings and classes and workshops and interviews, and generally not writing (because they don't have time), and also not being paid (by state statute, bewildering as that may be). Being poet laureate is a service of immense generosity.

And part of that generosity is here, in these poems they've shared with us all, these gems of nerve and pore and follicle, these lenses into the witnessed world. We at the Montana Arts Council are proud to present the work of our poets laureate, our honored ones, and to introduce to you poets and works you may not know are out there, simmering, waiting to show you something.

I hope you'll read with joy and curiosity, find something new and enlivening, and buy more books by these poets. Stack 'em up by your bedside. Wake up each day with a new poem. Memorize one while you climb the stairs. Fall in love with a few. Let the gods touch you, in some secret, permanent way.

Krys Holmes
Director, Montana Arts Council
July 2024

INTRODUCTION

In the spring of 2024, a few months into my term as poet laureate, I received a request for a phone interview from an East Coast journalist writing an article about poets laureate residing in rural states. Intrigued, and never shy about garnering more literary attention (not to mention being keenly aware of the unspoken mandate that these are the types of things a poet laureate *should* be agreeing to), I happily acquiesced to the interrogation. It didn't get off to the best start.

"Some people from other parts of the country," the interviewer began with, to my keen and ever-suspicious ears, a not-so-subtle hint of condescension, "might suggest that a state like Montana might not have much culture. What do you have to say about that?" I paused, a little stunned, then sputtered something about "morons" bookended by a choice expletive or two; I'll skip the specifics. Perhaps not the best way to earn the heart and mind of someone originally from Massachusetts, but hey, they asked for it. I got through the interview, though I have only the vaguest recollection of what else we talked about; for the rest of the way I was trying to interact through a brain mostly hissing with the harsh tone of a television test pattern the likes of which we don't really get to wake up to on the couch in the wee hours of the night anymore.

So, no culture? In Montana? Where do I begin?! I'll start with the gorgeous and vibrant millennias-old cultures of the dozen Indigenous tribes forced to live inside arbitrary boundaries within the borders of this so-called state. The startling differences among them and the equally startling similarities. The art, music, and, especially, storytelling traditions. The traditional ways of living on and with the land that I can't describe as anything less than poetic. Everything in our state begins here and it is part of all of our lives every day, whether you recognize it or not. It is a beautiful history and a bloody and terrible one and it absolutely shapes us.

Don't just take it from me. Great Falls writer and historian Joseph Kinsey Howard writes in his 1943 masterpiece *Montana: High, Wide, and Handsome* that "the degree of man's culture may be measured by the efficiency of his integration with his environment." That Montana culture, he figures, must then "effect a synthesis of all those which have gone before." Howard grounds his idea of the state's defining traits in Montana's Native people, who "left Montanans a tradition of outdoor living, a regard for stamina and courage."

This is a perfect and necessary place to start. The Indigenous cultures are the seeds that nothing grows here without. Then there are the introduced cultures from the multitudes of people who have found their way here from all over the world. The kinship networks that grew because of them. The languages and traditions and ways of being, and how they have morphed and interacted to create such a rich atmosphere for those of us who live here today. And then of course the vast breadth of humanity here too that historians like Howard have generally failed to mention, in all its magnificent sexual and gender and religious and multi-spirited fluidity that can turn a dreary downtown street into a joyous explosion of color and music just because someone had the brilliant idea to throw a parade. Nothing truly melts here but plenty blooms, and it all jockeys and wrassles for position and incorporates this and sets aside that. Everything we make and do grows from this ancient soil made rich with tears of joy and sorrow. What good fortune that we get to experience it all, in this wondrous place, together.

The poets appearing between the covers of this book are an excellent example of the diversity of expression that the vast breadth of cultural origins in Montana can evoke from the spirits of the people paying closest attention. There have been eleven of us, and I am the third Indigenous person to occupy this lofty position. By the time this book hits shelves we will be lumbering toward a twelfth poet laureate and, given the certainty of this anthology staying in print for a long, long time, there might have even been thirteen or fourteen or fifteen and certainly more Indigenous poets laureate since. There could be an entirely new anthology of the second wave underway! This book is merely a beginning to, and a continuation of, a long spiraling tradition of expression through words of what it's like to be alive here. Words on a page, or words spoken from-hush-to-bellow around a campfire.

And who better than poets to show us what it's like to live here, to love here, to struggle here, to survive here? To be in community here! To show us what it's like to express who we are here. In that respect, this book is a celebration of Being here! And we, all of us poets, are grateful to have you here with us.

Chris La Tray
11th Montana State Poet Laureate
Ode'imini-giizis (Strawberry Moon), June 2024

MONTANA'S POETS LAUREATE

2005–2025

SANDRA ALCOSSER

2005–2007

Sandra Alcosser's poems have appeared in the *New Yorker,* the *New York Times, Paris Review, Ploughshares, Poetry*, and the *Pushcart Prize Anthology.* She received two individual artist fellowships from the National Endowment for the Arts, and her books of poetry, *A Fish to Feed All Hunger* and *Except by Nature,* received the highest honors from the National Poetry Series, the Academy of American Poets, and associated writing programs, as well as the Larry Levis Award and the William Stafford Award for Poetry. Her four artist book collaborations with Brighton Press have been exhibited internationally and reside in museums and special collections including the National Museum of Women in the Arts and Musee d'art Americain Giverny. She was the National Endowment for the Arts' first Conservation Poet for the Wildlife Conservation Society and Poets House, New York, as well as Montana's first poet laureate and recipient of the Merriam Award for Distinguished Contribution to Montana Literature. She founded and directs San Diego State University's Master of Fine Arts Program each fall and serves as editor-in-chief of *Poetry International.*

BEGIN AGAIN

Because of open woodland
With quivering sun patches

A bird's eye might observe a worm
Chiseling under earth's

Skin—because of granite boulders
Full of egg cases holding

Spiderlings—because of purple berries
Come sweet in July—chokecherry

Shadblow Nanking
Hips and haws ripening—

Branch nesters build summer nurseries
On the face of our cabin—the same family

Each year or their progeny
On ridgepole—purlin—crossbeam

Sensitive to every human gesture
Inside the window and when men

Come to paint the fascia or spray
The log base and its foundation

The nester will abandon her clutch
Of eggs—blued by mineral blood—

Begin to weave a new nest
High above squirrels and house cats

For aren't we all pattern-making animals—
Make a beautiful thing and you've done all you can

To battle a friend said to me
And a people-adapted species—

Nuthatch or chickadee or these
Robins—become a kind of mother country—

Like you dear America—offering a body each day
For someone to make a waste land—

I would like to weave with the surety
Of that robin—only a heartbeat

And a wrist wing to shape her nest—
A shaggy cup of mud and spider web

Come greed come windstorm—begin again

MOTHERS

From under water and under tar,
Down from the walls of caves
They came. The biologist made
A circle with her arms
That calf's heart must have weighed
Twenty-five pounds she said. *Deep inside*
Each bison there is a bible,
Otherwise how could they survive
Our bullets and cliffs
Our cities and flames
Our soups simmering
With the heads of their babies
Each mother grazing patiently—
A ton of flesh made of grass blades

IMAGO

I know where the mourning cloak
Butterflies come from I know where they go
I say to my beautiful black-Irish friend
As we lunch in a cavernous Palladian
Café where moments ago she closed
Her eyes and rubbed her palms together
As I asked about her happiest moment so
Far this year—She'd driven up the coast
From LA in a brand new sea foam
Fiat and she mouths its color—*Verde Chiaro*
Her first new car ever—She'd stopped and rested
Each evening at the home of an old lover or friend
And she speaks of them now with such tenderness—
So begins the weave—I tell her how I came upon them—
The cloaks—on a path beside the cabin
Two-inch black white and red harlequin
Caterpillars that left the willow sapling stripped
And when I craned above the branch they bristled
Vibrated *en masse* like an imperial dragon
Greatly overestimating my stature—
My friend looks with vague curiosity—
Human conversation always a halting melody for me
But I try to match her happiness with the levity
Of the butterflies—their puddling and basking
Didn't Nabokov describe discovering them
As the most intense pleasure known to men—
Comparing a mourning cloak to his first lover
a dark rustling path where she gripped him *by the shoulder*
rubbed her sand-dusted shoe against the stocking of her other
leg higher up under the hem
Behind us on the almost-summer terrace
Sweeping in like aesthetes just as the lilacs surrender
Their lush perfume the western tiger swallowtails

Jink down through the trees
Descend and slip their long tongues and yellow bodies
Into the lavender bloom
Too much to bear—this delicious afternoon
Though we used to be at the age of weddings—my friend
And I—then baby showers, and soon enough—vanishing
While all about the spectacles—the grand sipping and bliss
The wonder of the country in the denuded willow
And the city full of seductive roads
Like jelly without shape slowly we
Approach the next stage—*Imago*—Linneus
Called it when gelatin takes
Off its mask to become the perfect image of its species

GREG PAPE

2007–2009

Greg Pape is the author of *A Field of First Things, Four Swans, Animal Time, American Flamingo* (Crab Orchard Open Competition Award), *Sunflower Facing the Sun* (Edwin Ford Piper Prize, now called the Iowa Prize), *Storm Pattern, Black Branches, Border Crossings* (Pitt Poetry Series), and other books. His work has received the Discovery/*The Nation* Award, two National Endowment for the Arts Individual Fellowships, the Richard Hugo Memorial Poetry Award, the Pushcart Prize, and other awards. His poems have appeared in the *Atlantic, Colorado Review, Cutbank, Field,* the *Florida Review, Iowa Review, Literary Accents,* the *Louisville Review, Miramar,* the *New Yorker, Poetry, Kyoto Journal,* and others. He is professor emeritus at the University of Montana, where he taught writing from 1987 to 2016. He currently serves on the faculty in Spalding University's Naslund-Mann School of Writing. He has an MFA degree from the University of Arizona and an MA from California State University, Fresno. Pape has taught literature and writing at Hollins University, the University of Missouri, the University of Alabama, where he served as the Coal Royalty Chair in poetry, the University of Louisville, where he served as Bingham Poet-in-Residence, Northern Arizona University, Florida International University, and elsewhere. He has been awarded fellowships at the Fine Arts Work Center in Provincetown, Massachusetts, the Centrum Foundation at Fort Worden State Park in Washington, and the Bread Loaf Writers' Conference in Middlebury, Vermont, where he was a Robert Frost Fellow. He has read his work nationwide and in Canada, Mexico, Italy, and Japan. His poetry reflects a deep appreciation for diverse landscapes and people, a love of animals, and an attentiveness to the natural world, which of course includes the man-made world. He divides his time between the Bitterroot Valley in Montana, where he is a founding member of the Bitterroot River Protection Association, and Frankfort, Kentucky. He is currently at work on a new book of poems and a memoir.

TRACKS & TRACES

Slabs of ice covered with snow
and the tracks of an otter who came ashore
and bounded along a curved path
for fifty feet and lowered its tail
and slid back into the water.
It must be fun to be an otter.
Farther on, tracks of a couple dozen geese
who'd had a meeting on the ice.
It must have been cordial, no one
stepped in another's tracks, and it must
have ended suddenly with them all
lifting at once into the air.
Wouldn't that be something, to bend
your knees, to raise your arms
and spread your feathers and pull them
down and push off your webbed feet
and stretch out your long neck
and lift off into the air above the river
with a bunch of friends honking and barking
and lining up in a pattern that made sense
to everyone and seemed to ennoble the air?
Well, watch out for your lost brother
down there in the tules, calling and calling,
over here over here. His love is tender
and violent and hard to explain.
Brother goose, sister otter forgive us our ways.
We'll all sleep together, as T'ao Ch'ien said,
a bent arm on the pillow, keeping emptiness whole.

I go on walking, glancing down to see the path,
then up into the trees to see the trees, owls
maybe, great-horned, long-eared, saw-whet,
woodpeckers, hairy, downy, pileated,

the brown creeper, the snipe, or porcupines,
those shy four-footed cacti of the north woods
who gnaw the bark and sweet cambium
of the young pines and climb higher
than the owls roost to roll up into a ball
of quills and sleep away the cold
like that old Buddhist monk called Bird's Nest
because he liked to sleep and meditate in the trees.

When I see one I bow backwards and gaze awhile
in porcupine time. Then I walk on, step over
a fallen branch, a rock. I walk until the path
fades and my steps find their way to a huge
uprooted Ponderosa pine wind tore loose
and lay down, leaving a cleft, a hole I step
down into, roots and rootlets still holding,
dangling in constellations, the rounded river stones
they clung to when the big wind came down
through Kootenai Canyon—a time of violence
become a place of shelter, part of the story
that houses us all.

THE WOOLY MAMMOTHS

What happened to the wooly mammoths?
We ate them, and they became us?
We had thought that early hunters,
after the invention of the atlatl and lethal
Clovis spear-point, killed off the wooly mammoths,
hunted them into extinction, along
with the saber-tooth tigers. Even the giant
armadillos could have succumbed
to the hunter's spear and cunning.
Isn't it a wonder the wooly mammoth
is much beloved among humans
who have never seen one except
in artist's re-creations and bones
wired together in museums?
Those great aunts and uncles of the elephants
with their marvelous tusks and hilly demeanors
still roam the plains and vast interiors
of human dreamscapes. Now,
from fragments found in dry riverbeds
and lines of interstellar dust in the melting
glaciers, we've pieced together
a new theory of the mammoth's extinction.
It wasn't our spears but meteors laced
with minute diamonds unlike any jewels
of earth that rained from space
and set the land on fire.
If we have a picture, if we can smell
the earth, if we know hunger, if fire
has warmed us, if wind has cooled us,
if we have listened to water
and considered starlight, we can honor
the mammoths still roaming inside us,
we can make a story like a bowl from shards.

THE SPELL OF THE BITTERROOT

Our river runs north, map-wise anyway,
but it has been ditched and diked,
riprapped and rerouted,
dredged and diverted,
channelized, head-gated, and privatized
in many places. Portages abound,
and no-trespassing signs hang from strands
of barb-wire strung across braids.
This is not right.
But does the river care? It just wants
to meander, take its own sweet time,
trust in gravity and the tidal pull
of eventual dissolution
in the great peace-making sea.
As Vernon Woolsey, our deceased water master
who drifts now in that sea, certainly well knew,
any shoring-up or riprapping the banks
will have consequences downstream.
Sometimes it seems history
is simply a string of bad ideas,
like lining the banks of the river
with wrecked cars.
A pristine trout stream
sandwiched between two lanes
of the stalled traffic of the dead.
But then fenders, hoods, and mangled grills
broke loose from the cables,
batteries wept acid over the stones,
headlights and windshields ground
into a kind of sand, and the sleek coupes
and sedans of lost decades
littered the bars and beaches.
Progenitor of the caddis and stonefly,

the midge and the trout, our river
runs under the spell of anastomosis;
from the Greek for opening,
ana, throughout, and stoma, mouth;
a mouth that won't stay closed,
a network of living vessels, veins
in a watery leaf of earth,
channels, braids, a continuous flow
of wild water. Just as we do,
our river wants to stretch out
and move freely in its own bed.

HENRY REAL BIRD

2009–2011

Henry Real Bird grew up on the Crow Reservation, ranching with his grandparents, and spoke only Apsáalooke upon entering first grade. Henry competed in saddle bronc riding in college and rode professionally on the PRCA circuit from 1973–1980 until an injury propelled him out of the saddle and into writing. He earned a bachelor's degree in elementary education from MSU-Bozeman and his master's at MSU-Billings, and has since written two collections of poetry, *Wolf Teeth* and *Horse Tracks,* as well as six anthologies and a dozen children's books. Published by Lost Horse Press, *Horse Tracks* was named the 2011 Poetry Book of the Year by the High Plains Book Awards.

Named the third Montana poet laureate in 2009, the following summer Henry traveled the state's northern plains on horseback, handing out books of poetry from the saddle as he went, following paths ridden by his grandfather and great-grandfather. Speaking of the landscape, he told *NPR's* Michele Norris: "It's so big that you can't really put an edge to it. That's how it is today in a vast sea of buffalo grass."

In addition to writing poetry, Henry has taught reading at all elementary school grades and has also served on the Montana Advisory Committee on Children and Youth and the Crow Central Education Commission. In partnership with Karen Stone and Joseph Coburn he developed the Indian Reading Series, a reading and language development program. Featuring Henry's stories written in both Crow and English, the series helps students at twelve Native American reservations in the Northwest learn and preserve the Crow language, a vital part of passing Apsáalooke tradition and culture on to future generations. Henry is a spiritual person who attained mysticism numerous times from fasting and vision quests, and still lives by the sacred pipe.

ODD NUMBERED GEESE

Can't really do much of anything
As salty sweat stains hardened on my pony,
Seems as if a big heavy rain
And light hail dropped on us.
The soaked terrain
Illuminated a pale-colored surface
Of ash stained lavender bluish layers.
Mother Earth cupped her hand
For the cowboy to ride through
The twilight in the breaks land.
A growing attitude,
The rhythm has to go where you want
Not where it may.
But until my memories go blind,
Why rope,
If you're not going to ride?
Why run the horses in
If you're not going to ride?
But may the horses return.
Odd numbered geese
Over Wolf Teeth
Cast feeling beneath.
My soul has gone east
To leave me sleepless.
The death of a feeling,
In the sunlight through the teepee's neck
The fine dust ascends gently.
Sparkling in the sunlight
Are my feelings.
For love stood still, alive in her tracks
In the sunlight to ascend gently
Through the teepee's neck.

RIVERS OF HORSE

All you real human beings, listen.
This is the story of the coming of the horse.
The Spanish barb the Comanche rode,
The mystic pony the Shoshone stole,
Drifting up from the Rio Grande
To the Columbia River Basin,
Mighty herds the Cayuse drove,
Mighty herds of horses.
Out of a dream they came to the Crow,
Sioux, Cheyenne and Arapaho,
Through the Northern Plains and mountains grazed,
Around the wolf and buffalo strayed,
Flowing herds of horses,
Rich flowing herds of horses.
Rivers of horse,
Rich rivers of horse,
Up and down these coulees and draws,
From the Rio Grande, the Platte
And the Powder River, flow herds,
Of this mystic pony,
Of this mystic pony.
Tapping willow stick, I can still hear,
I can still hear my grandfather
Tapping painted black with a willow stick.
At one time, a long time ago,
My Grandfather Owns Painted Horse
Behind him I sat
On his horse painted black,
I hugged him lightly
As I leaned the right side of my face
Gently against his back, These horses have a soul,
Do them good and respect them.
Talk good to them and they know.

They talk to each other, they say.
"When you talk good to the horse's spirit,
They will come to you, and you will be
Lucky with them in a heart that is good,"
Said my Grandfather Owns Painted Horse.
At the edge of my eye something went by,
It returned into my feeling,
You're so far away from me
As I stare into the twinkle and glitter
Of blowing snow flakes in the wind.
Before, the warrior was respected,
The hides on his lodge reflected
The quality of horses he rode,
Great horses made great warriors,
Atop a fast running buffalo horse
He could catch a fast running buffalo,
To stick an arrow behind the last rib
And deep into the heart.
The warrior's people ate the best of meat
Packed on his many horses.
The war horse was the most prized of steeds
Tied to his thigh as it grazed outside
The lodge by night. This was the war horse,
He used to strike the grand coup
As he ran up on the enemy to touch him
While he was still alive,
Many feathers of grand coup,
And return with many horses
Make for a long-tailed war bonnet.
Great horses made great warriors.
The second best coup
Was to enter the enemy camp by night,
To cut the rawhide rope attached
To the sleeping enemy warrior's top mount.
From a dream he was given this
White sorrel medicine horse paint

In the shadow of Shining Mountains,
In the moon of the first thunder
Atop his medicine horse paint, he could
Swoop up a beautiful woman to steal
From Lodges That Are Different from his.
His song they would sing
As he danced the scalp dance and the victory dance,
To give away the best of horses,
Fast running horses, to spread
Good fortune among his people,
He was close to the horse's spirit,
On the great war horse
He could kill the enemy,
Lead a successful war party,
To become the chief, the man that is good.
The Maker blessed him with great horses,
So he had someone to lean his back against.
The great horse made the warrior great.
Remembered pulling strands of sinew thread
To run through my mouth, to pinch one end,
Then to roll-twist the rest down the outside
Of my right thigh, on late snowy winter night.
I got up to poke the fire,
When Grandmother Everything She Joins
Recalled this story:
A horse that is good,
Their brother-in-law they would give
To show love and respect for their sister.
A girl's parents would give
Ten good horses to a great warrior
To marry their daughter.
But a man who is not a man
Would give horses to a girl's parents
For the girl's hand in marriage,
So the great warrior would have
Many horses and many wives.

Back when the woman lived with the man,
Before, that's how it was.
The children of a respectable family
Would ride Appaloosa horses
With no tails as a prestige symbol,
The rest of the old folk's horses,
And children's horses wore squared-off tails,
These great horses made people great
Out in the northern mountains and Plains,
Where horses and women were stolen
In intertribal Plains warfare.
Bird Horse, Horse On The Other Side,
Medicine Tail, Pretty Paint, Rides the Horse,
Takes the Horse, Horse Herder, Spotted Horse,
Brings Home Many Geldings, Has a Lot of Colts,
Lucky with His Horse, Always Rides Horses,
Gray Horse Rider, Sorrel Horse, Buckskin Horse,
Black Horse Rider, Lead Horse Rider:
These are our names from a horse culture.
Then, there was a day when all of my father's horses
Were killed by the Bureau of Indian Affairs,
And Sell Out Indians for twenty-five cents an ear.
So too with the coyote and magpie,
But they survived in time,
Before that, the buffalo and wolf were gone.
After this, the sheep and spotted buffalo
Were brought in to eat the buffalo grass,
"Don't shed a tear for the horses
For they replace a human being's life,"
Said my Grandmother Everything She Joins,
Florence Medicine Tail Real Bird,
"But that day, I made my tears drop
When they killed all the horses.
That day was bad, my heart was bad.
If these were days like those when lodges used to move,
My heart would be extremely good."

Painted Black Horse Rider, Spirit Horse Rider,
Protector and Defender of the Crow
Who still rides the prairies and mountains,
I have always been told about you.
So now I offer you Painted Black Horse Rider,
My sacred pipe for many good tomorrows.

EARTH DAY

Ice-backed, powder-snow-dusted longhorn cattle
Moving slowly in cold, dust-snowy morning
As I ride alone in your feeling.
I've been listening to the silence
Out among the Wolf Teeth.
You've touched my heart like the silent burst
Of shooting stars descending homeward
To our Mother Earth.
This morning I saw the horizon stretch
Over in the country where the Black Lodge hunt,
The spirit appeared to sun.
Just between you and me
I go dreaming beyond doubt, deep into a feeling.
The heathen Indian before beyond,
But past the reflection
Of a life he never knew.
After riding through the memories
In the nothingness of stories
Am I to exist merely as a question?
Your feelings resist, looking into a constellation
I forgot your memory last night.
Wolf pups frolicking in tall buffalo grass
But what is the connection?
Winds across the prairie blew
As the maggot tidies with his bite
From there commencing past the rot
Of a buffalo skull pure white?
The Indian licking institutional window glass
Of a life in fermentation.
Upon walking on
To the decomposed carcass of an Indian
Exhumed by the synthetic thrills and highs
Past the cold edges of oblivion

I know his soul till lies in the silent subconscious
Of a swindling, corrupt corporate lawyer
Walking down Fourteenth and K.
And yet there is another Indian
Sitting on the guard rail,
High flying feeling where I could hear
The beautiful voice of the woman in the drum
The spirit of love.
A kindly thunderous cloud snapping and cracking lightning
Way high in the light wind
Thunder and lightning, sunlight in the rain.
Just a-riding along
Looking at my long shadow on the ground
Just a-riding along
On up to the backwaters, to the still waters
Where the wind whistles on over the water
To show me the sacredness of life
As I begin to speak on behalf
Of the wind, water and our Mother Earth.
The so-called primitive environmentalist
Softened his Mother's heart
When his tears touched the ground,
And with his flesh-offering held high,
He began to speak with He Who First Did Everything,
"This earth, our Mother, watch her always."
The grass has reached its fullest length
And the sun is two fists high,
Within the clouds in the sun
Emerged a buffalo for strength
In the thunder and lightning of the sky
Blessed in thoughts for the sunshine in the rain
May you safely reach the spring rain
With visions of horses, and in my dream
This Spirit Being said,
"The horses have returned."
That is what I have asked for you,

That may you use,
And winters many may you see.
In my dream the horses came down Medicine Tail
And crossed the Little Big Horn River
On their home trail,
On our Sacred Mother Earth.

MASS IN CROW

Last night I was out with my buffalo brothers
In songs and prayers,
Where colors swirled and sparkled.
To his death
Columbus thought he had discovered Asia.
Jesus was crucified
And Nixon saw impeachment.
Open pit mining left tailings bleached
To blast your sight.
They poisoned and polluted
The virgin pure waters.
Buffalo ate the grass,
Barbwire was in his stomach.
Birds use shredded threads of nylon tarps
Instead of horse hair for nests.
Farm boys who once cleared fields of rocks
Now make a trail of rocks in fields
For center-pivot irrigation system tires.

The moon and sun move around the teepee
As we smoke with the ground
And feed the water
In cosmic universal alliance walk.

Oedipus Rex, archway to the West,
The wolf dog barks and growls at the dark,
Polyphonic politician mumbles riddles,
But we dry the wild turnips and wild carrots
To walk toward another winter.
Mass is in Crow and Indian ceremonies in English
Self foe society fights for a better reclamation
Cattle now graze in sight of dragline.
As a better moon is rising
We recognize the person whispering to the horse.

The moon and sun move around the teepee
As we smoke with the ground
And feed the water
In cosmic universal alliance walk.

SHERYL NOETHE

2011–2013

For Sheryl's biographical information, see "Ides of March," page 30.

IN YOUR SLEEP

So if you die in your sleep-
Ing mind
Every new day is the hereafter.

Empires burn, nations, cities,
Mountain ranges and forests,
Entire civilizations

Rebuilt every night a trillion times.
The bits that fit together, stars and blood cells
Across dimensions regardless of measure

Or passage of time, indefinite and continuing
The contoured shapes of events and existence
In the past, present and future as a whole.

If you can climb to the top, you can see paradise
Where life is thin, and death is the price of admission.

I want to see every great city from above
I want to be astonished.

WHORE

1
The most beautiful woman in the world remains faceless,
back-lit by a burning city in the Palatial Era,
where the most admired and despised queen
of the Bronze Age would not stay in her husband's bed but instead
sailed across the Aegean Sea with Sweet Paris.
Some say she left her palace willingly.
In one version a king claimed that she was
Instead hiding in Egypt for the duration.

2
Helen was blamed here for the separation of Asia and Europe.
Men celebrated in calling her *whore, harlot, adulterer, vagabond.*
They said of Helen: *Her smile has been paid for.*
Indifferent, unsure of her wishes, wrote the poets.
Her Trojan husband said irresistible longings lay him low.
A gold ring in a swine's snout they called her, said,
The silver glints of her earrings could catch the heart.
Her braids shined down from her deathless head.
The sight of her weakened men's knees.
She was spell-binding in a superstitious age
Seeing her soft face annihilated resistance or logic.
Now a fixture in the quantification of beauty,
the contests began here and continue, long after death
Helen became a blueprint for Western society.
Always at the heart of the interrogation, bleeding beyond scenes.
They said she caused the rift between Europe and Asia.

Greeks assembled twelve-hundred ships and thousands:
Achaeans; Athenian, Spartan, Theban, set off to Troy.
Seeking favorable winds, the king sacrificed his own daughter.
Achilles tried but couldn't rescue the young princess Iphigenia,
Butchered like a goat, face-down on the altar.
Immediately afterward the breezes turned to gusts,
Blasting gales of fury to propel the men toward death.
Gods and heroes took sides, spurred the blood-letting.
The goddess of beauty fevered the warriors, roused them madly.

2
We danced, led by the beautiful buttocks of Aphrodite.
Hours of darkness more melting than sleep, nor sweet in vain.

3
In the theatre Helen was portrayed by a naked man.
Aptly named, Hell; for men and ships and cities.
She distracted them from their linear development.
A man making love, she said, cannot fight.

4
Culture is a living surface from which we pull
the bodies of the drowned.
We were about to carry out our plans,
if not for the shipwreck.

5
Helen married the god Apollo once they were both dead.

IDES OF MARCH

We
The Venezuelan couple, illegal, sleek and chic as King Cobras,
Proposed marriage to Wiley Coyote and me in order to get green cards.
Lots of careless money, parties, travel, and a fabulous loft to share.
She was an exotic stuffed silk suit on a coiled body with a temper,
so glamorous, undulating her amazing form across the dance floor.
Her dark Brazilian beauty drew long looks from other men.
She was armed with that husband; an importer (he said)
We considered it, glamorized from cocaine, the bigger life: swank,
Illicit continental encounters, bigger deals, beautiful furniture,
Fancy clothes, and excitement in our glamorous gypsy ways,
In reptile-skin fuck-me boots, stilettos, sharp heels
Chasing the dragon and got swallowed. *Now he won't pay*
any attention to me. He doesn't appear to hear. He's out of focus.
The sharp smell of cannabis, carnal bliss, getting pissed.
I loved walking into lower east-side bars and being greeted by hard
dapper men emanating danger.
        "Jose" I whispered, "I can't wake him up!" and he pulled me
        close into his arms and kissed my neck,
        "You're his woman. You take care of him. Entiendas?"
He
Travels now through old buildings, industrial ruins,
Abandoned factories, climbs behind scaffolding, snakes across
Pipes damp with condensation, gets a foothold with his sneakers.
Slides between the sheet-rock, around the studs, eaves and rafters,
Between particles of matter and then he's gone.
Not worth a mention, Stoop-shouldered, hunched in shame
He slips through the place in his hood, slouching, anonymous
In the back near the exit door; unkempt, dirty, bangs over his face,
Thinning hair combed carefully forward. What must he suffer,
Longing for the vast wealth he was entitled to, the family fortune
He expected from his grandmother, the elegant and privileged
Old woman who clearly preferred him of all the six brothers,

Taught him to be a snob, to select expensive Champagne,
And to look at other people as classes.
He included himself in the elite although he rarely held a job.
Wheedles and sidles and smiles, handing out the forbidden
From his crooked hands, reminders of serious mistakes,
Brutality in his youth with the drug cartels before anyone
knew the names of the places, and they set the Gringo up for arrest.
Hiding at home where his brother *ratted him out,*
He claimed, and so he slammed the garage door
on his sibling's feet, breaking them, flattening the arches.
He made a woman dangerous. As police hauled him
Off to prison she ran wildly after them down the street screaming.
Living in abandoned housing, she hung world-maps
Over the holes in the plaster.
Later I heard about the shoplifting,
The boyfriend/heroin addict/burglar.
The youngest boy stood, folding fresh pasta ribbons
Over a wooden broom handle, his brother's eyes looking
Out at me, and with the brother's mouth as he told me
How he watched his brother addle a woman, madden her,
Intent only upon what their bodies could do, deathly passion,
Surprising, without name or precedent. Outlaws in bad traffic,
Intercepting the other's thoughts in a glance, a nod
She gave him her body then she gave up.

Me
He took me through infuriating situations: dinner at a drug house,
Birthday party with a former mob guy, kneecapped
Over a small error, dinners with punk rockers and celebrities,
MTV spokes models, vain and dismissive Europeans.
Lethal drug connections.
At the insistence of the crack-head wife
We celebrated our upcoming birthdays.
I'd never seen her so excited. "Fiesta Saggitariana!"
Clapping her hands, "Fiesta!"
The four of us sat down in the tiny kitchen. She pulled a foil tray

Of frozen lasagna from the stove, edges burned, icy at the center,
Tossed it disinterestedly onto the table where we waited
With our paper plates. I pulled a foot-long black hair from
A miserable salad of soggy lettuce and pale tomatoes,
Saturated with dressing. No one else was interested in eating.
We gave up on the illusion.
We forgot the table and hustled into the room with the pipe and the rock.
A mock household: bunk beds, a lit bowl, two-dozen dead bolt locks,
Kool-Aid cups, plastic soldiers, toy cars and uncle banging around
With hinges in his legs, a dirty green couch with cigarette burns,
Nightmare cartoon propelled by crank peopled by two little sons;
Sweet and delicate, frail and dark-eyed, terribly thin.
Barely cared for. I'd seen children like this in institutions,
Damaged by the place itself. The youngest boy's neck was weak,
His large head lolled, he was clumsy and slow,
Thrilled to show his cars to me, I guessed he was about three or four,
but the mother said he was in second grade. I looked at
My companion, face tight as a brick, and after a number
Of hours a car service finally came to drive us back to the city,
Twitching and tweaking as our synapses for joy prickled,
Blinked out.
What about those kids I asked
What about them he said
Are they getting help in school? What do you think?
He asked
Sounding surprised
That anyone has time to care about them?

She

The woman's name was Maya. Scandinavian, pale and roseate,
With silken white hair in a bob. She was extremely, exquisitely
Dreamy, feral, and reckless: jumping off bridges into rivers,
On the run, eluding the police. It was minor stuff, until
He taught her what he knew, by instinct. Intense sex;
Class-one pharmaceuticals. His smooth unlined body,
Unconscious musculature of a boy, slim, and taut, veined.

He taught her about the limbus between pleasure and pain,
Even confusing the two in their willingness.
The kind of play that pulls at a woman relentlessly,
Insistent, pulling her apart, pushing her together,
In fever and desperation
No one will ever be able to do this again. She is spoiled.
Her succubus was a living man. An opportunist who could
Never get enough; always choosing the path of least resistance.
He considered himself extremely clever. Wily, he called it.
Yet when it came to the emotional expression, he was mute,
Uninterested in making, or naming, or giving, which he did not do.
Without mission or avocation, his ghost had a withered arm.
He focused on hedonism and sensuality, gourmet food,
Expensive wines, estates and yachts and heiresses, he loved
to describe his spectacular friends: the most beautiful women
Celebrities, punk-rock bands, yacht racers, models,
Children of wealth, connoisseurs, racketeers, entrepreneurs,
Smugglers, wealth. Always, in the end, alone.
He obtained whatever was trending in the market for pharmacopoeia.
Thus he met greats of music, well-known actors, politicians' kids,
French girls. He knew one with a platinum Mohawk, platform shoes,
Teeny tiny skirts and the most fabulous t-shirts and furs,
Torn fishnet stockings and drooping silk slips. Her name was GiGi.
She only wanted his drugs as well as the heiress
With Marilyn Monroe leanings, moles in the right places,
Cleavage everywhere, breathy little voice, blinking and flirting for favor.
Leather pants and biker jacket-clad girls friendly as far as the product.
They showed up, fake kissing, fraudulent enthusiasm,
When he introduced them as friends, they had a hard time
Keeping a straight face for long. Their eyes roamed the room for a get-high.
He was a drunk and a wine snob, although when it got bad
He poured bottles of any sort down his throat. He paraded
Girl after girl past me, giving the impression that not only
Were they the best of friends, deeply treasured,
Also he'd likely had sex with all of them
before blacking out for the next twenty-some hours.

TAMI HAALAND

2013–2015

Tami Haaland is the author of four collections of poetry, *If I Had Said Beauty, What Does Not Return, When We Wake in the Night,* and *Breath in Every Room.* Her poems have appeared in *Fugue, Cutthroat,* the *American Journal of Poetry, december, The Ecopoetry Anthology,* and *Cascadia,* and have been featured on the *Writer's Almanac, Verse Daily, American Life in Poetry,* and the *Slowdown.* She was born on the Hi-Line and lives in Billings.

SHE WAS SO TINY

She was so tiny I would give her anything:
sweets, cinnamon or lemon, thick puddings,
strawberries. I would give her my arm, a smile,
kisses on the forehead, my rocking frame beside her.
I said it was okay. Wasn't it? I said I loved her
and rubbed her bony back, her swollen feet.
We would play with lipstick and lotions.
Your dry skin, I'd say. Her hair, the brush,
the silly way they would braid her into a girl
but I wanted her hair long and loose, waves
spilling down her neck. Her sunken eyes, her warnings,
go now. Her greetings, you're finally here.

It was a long while and it was yesterday.
It was a year and a mile, a daily escape,
a treat, a burden, a weight. We walked
to the exotic swans and watched them preen.
We compared shoes and traded clothes. We had
sunlight, we had the gorgeous single red poppy in weeds,
we had a back fence we couldn't climb,
unplanted flowerbeds, cigarette butts
heeled into sidewalks. What a place.
We were somebody's sister or another's enemy.
Sometimes they hadn't seen us for years,
and we watched them make bright forests
on paper using glitter to imitate the sky.

A COLANDER OF BARLEY

The smell, once water has rinsed it,
is like a field of ripe grain, or the grain held
in a truck, and if you climb the steel side,
one foot lodged on the hubcap, the other
on the wheel, and pull your body upward,
your hands holding to tarp hooks, and lift toes
onto the rim of the truck box, rest your ribs
against the side, you will see beetles
and grasshoppers among the hulled kernels.
Water stirs and resurrects harvest dust:
sun beating on abundance, the moist heat
of grain collected in steel, hands
plunging and lifting, the grain spilling back.

DEER ON CRAZY CREEK

Along the trail I think how risky the venture,
the signs that say don't go alone into bear country.
I can see miles except in aspen. Walking uphill
in sage I think of Yellow Woman, of the stranger
who finds her and takes her into another life.
It's after that, after coming from a grove of trees,
I climb on a huge split boulder and watch
an ant navigate a forest of lichens. When I
raise my eyes to the horizon, I see you,
the way you hold your head, ambling
along the trail, the sway of your body on this
path made long before humans managed and
mapped this place. You are doing what we do:
head down, step ahead, step ahead.
When you look up and I begin to speak, you stop,
deciding whether to bolt or continue, a turn
for us both. I wonder, do your thoughts go
to the bear at the edge of the mind, the long trail
with golden butterflies on sage, flies that chase
and bite? Do you understand what calls
and calls again from an aspen horizon?

MICHAEL EARL CRAIG

2015–2017

Michael Earl Craig is the author of *Iggy Horse* (2023), *Woods and Clouds Interchangeable* (2019), *Talkativeness* (2014), *Thin Kimono* (2010), *Yes, Master* (2006), *Can You Relax in My House* (2002), and the chapbook *Jombang Jet* (2011). He's published poems in various magazines, journals and anthologies—*Poetry,* the *Believer,* the *New Yorker* and the *Best American Poetry* (2014, 2022) among them. He was poet laureate for the State of Montana (2015–2017) and a Civitella Ranieri Foundation fellow (Fall 2021). He lives in the Shields Valley where he shoes horses for a living.

Originally an Ohioan—a Buckeye—it was my job, thirty-four years ago, to roam the west looking for an English department. I drove and took trains, looking at schools in Colorado, Oregon, Washington, and, the last stop on my list—Missoula, Montana. I drove into Missoula late afternoon fall of 1990 and by breakfast—at the Ox—I had found a new home. Something about Missoula just clicked. It felt raw and wild. I've written poems in a lot of different places since then, but Missoula in the early nineties was a magical town for me. Some people say that poetry matters because nothing depends on it. Others say poets are born, not paid. Or: Never ask a poet if they think you need a haircut.

But I digress. Thanks Montana for being the raw and wild green light that tipped me toward poetry. I won't forget it.

THE TRAIN

I have a cheese sandwich in my briefcase.
No one here understands me.
The conductor makes his rounds,
wants my foot out of the aisle.
Taps foot twice with clipboard.
Then smacks foot pretty hard.

I need ice for my apple juice.
They found a gas leak in the snack car.
Cold blue rails take me toward you
as unattended pugs roam
car to car looking for something.

Daybreak; I head for the dining car.
They seat me with a stranger.
He tells me he's seven—says
he's an orphan. I order French toast
with sausage links and a side of bacon.
He orders the fruit cup with herbal tea.
At which point his parents arrive,
have been looking for him for an hour.
His mother is stone faced. The father
begins to cry. The boy scoots over
and pats the bench seat beside him.

PREPARING TO PAINT THE BODY OF THE DEAD CHRIST IN THE TOMB

Did he think of himself that way,
as Hans Holbein the Younger,
standing yawning in the mirror?
He looked a little longer than usual,
then built up his bowl of pearled foam
and began to shave.

He'd ordered a corpse, it was on its way.
Fished from the Rhine
and he'd asked for a ripe one.

There was a horse, a horseman,
a long rope, a corpse
hauled onto the riverbank,
a running bowline tossed casually
around an ankle. The long rope
then tied to the saddle with
a gentle word or two for the horse,
a dirt-caked Friesian named Samuel
who misunderstood and began galloping.

As Hans shaved thoughtfully
beneath each nostril—
the horseman left standing
at the river—
this Samuel ran
as only a confused horse could
up the wet stone road,
into and through town,
dragging the tethered corpse

which leaked water and banged
disturbingly on the corners of buildings.
It went on for a while.

And because we believe
in poetry and uncanny timing,
it was precisely as Hans arrived
downstairs and stepped out
onto the front stoop
that this Samuel showed up
in a dash and braked—
a kind of sideways hockey-stop—

which brought the corpse
around nicely (albeit abruptly)
to the bare and bony feet of
the clean-shaven Holbein.

HE QUICKLY TOLD HIS LIFE STORY

A man was out back country skiing when he fell
and did something, broke something,
and he couldn't get up.

He lay there in the snow, miles from any road.
His dog was with him and as he lay there, this dog
raced about and snapped at the snow
and hopped over the man once, twice.
The man spoke to the dog but the dog did not recognize him.
Did not, the man sensed, seem to recognize him.

It was cold and getting dark.
The man could not feel his legs.
The dog was there, he barked insanely at a squirrel.
The man called the dog's name, ordered the dog to sit.
The man asked the dog to please come to him.

As darkness fell the man wondered if this was Death.
The dog was gone. The man lay on his back and cursed.
It was night.

Hours passed. The man thought he heard something.
The beam of a flashlight came stabbing at the trees.
It was his wife, she'd come upon him in the snow.
When he saw her he cried out. She knelt beside him
and he quickly recounted for her his life story
starting with the birthing canal, his first blankets—
then the sun, how it warmed the universe—
jobs he'd loved and hated—his golf clubs—his marriage—
a couple of cars he'd owned.
He blinked his eyes. He was angry.

The man raved but was alone. There was no one.
His limbs went out like candlewicks and he felt a flame
glowing in his chest. The dog ran like mad through the woods,
snapping at the wind.

LOWELL JAEGER

2017–2019

Lowell Jaeger is founding editor of Many Voices Press and editor of *New Poets of the American West*—an anthology of poets from eleven western states. Lowell has taught writing classes at numerous conferences and workshops and is currently professor of English/creative writing at Flathead Valley Community College (Kalispell, Montana), where he also served as Humanities Division Chair. He is a graduate of the Iowa Writer's Workshop, winner of the Grolier Poetry Peace Prize, and recipient of fellowships from the National Endowment for the Arts and the Montana Arts Council. Lowell was awarded the Montana Governor's Humanities Award for his work in promoting civil civic discourse. He is the author of nine collections of poems, the most recent of which are *Earth-blood & Star-shine* (Shabda Press, 2018) and *Ice Fishing with Fourth Graders* (Shabda Press, 2022).

POET LAUREATE, WHAT'S THAT?

Two years as Montana poet laureate and I've learned this: The Treasure State is rich with surprising landscapes and richer still with welcoming towns and lively minds. Each byway and back road leads to aesthetic pleasures of its own—antelope nesting in prairie grass while horses graze nearby, whitewater singing and cascading beneath thorny devil's club, breathtaking vistas of massive granite slabs aspiring skyward. So many Main Streets—some bustling with ranchers loading pickup beds with fence poles and spools of barbed wire, some crowded with souvenir shops and tourists sipping lattes and licking gelatos, some drowsy and half dreaming with dusty curbsides and empty storefronts and outlaw tumbleweed forever blowing in and out of town—but each of them with a poster in the hardware store or the post office or the pub, inviting townsfolk to meet the Montana poet laureate for an evening of cookies and laughter and thoughtful conversation.

My mind has been educated, my heart enriched, by shaking hands and listening to strangers' stories and sharing tales of my own. People asked: "Poet laureate, what's that?" I'm an ambassador for the arts, I told them. We need food and shelter and occupation, I'd explain; these we need to survive. But we also need to nourish our hearts and minds with the arts; these we need to truly thrive. Sure, that answer sounds highfalutin'. Reader, don't underestimate whatever it is within each of us—across race, gender, age, rank, and economic status—that looks up into the night sky and longs to understand the stars. Ask anyone who is willing to sit with you awhile, "What does it mean to be human?" Even grade-schoolers want to know. Now offer them a poem. Offer them a painting. Offer them music, dance, and a chance to shape clay with their hands. Whatever it is in each of us which longs for more than digging roots and keeping the cave lit with fire . . . well, that's where art comes from.

One inquisitive face or another asked me, "What is poetry?" In my younger days I'd parry the question by telling the story of Louis Armstrong. "What is jazz?" someone asked Armstrong. He famously responded, "If you need to ask that question you'll never know the answer." For years I considered this a wise and witty retort, but now as poet laureate, I looked into sincere faces asking an honorable question, and the Armstrong anecdote no longer served. I wanted to let people in, not lock people out. I was stung, a bit tongue-tied, to realize I had no worthy reply. In this way my audience educated me, prompted me to reflect and grow. Poetry, I learned to say, with a nod to Sir Ken Robinson, . . . is an "anti-anesthetic." Of course we need anesthetics for surgeries and other emergencies to numb the senses and dull the mind. Poetry (and all the arts!) strives to do the opposite: Poetry wants to enliven the senses and awaken the mind. This became my main message.

On a grey winter morning in Sydney, Montana, a bespectacled third grader waited patiently to speak with me after my presentation. He high-fived me, his eyes beaming with glee, and said, "O-S-U-M!" Then he turned and ran off. It took me a while, but later I decoded his compliment: "Awesome." He was a creative speller, a kindred spirit, thanking his lucky stars his morning had been memorable. Because of him, so had mine.

I named my poet laureate project "Poetry 101"—aiming to bring poetry to 101 venues in "all four corners" of Montana in two years. Well . . . I learned there were a lot more than four corners; I completed 156 events—some to crowds in auditoriums, some to a humble gathering of grateful ranch wives on folding chairs in the library basement. I've served many eager audiences. And that's what it all about—isn't it?—service. I've been honored to serve.

ELK

Count the tines on the rack,
head mounted on the wall.
Marlboro haze, pool ball clack,
shouts and laughter crowd the hall.

Now my gut aches me back
to a frosted sunrise, alpine grove.
A bull's bugle echoes rock
to rock, lifts to crags above

and blue beyond. Little ear
of each aspen leaf a-jingle.
I'm crouched, struck dumb. So near
the beast, my neck hairs tingle

as he snorts, stomps, struts, blows
his regal call. Someone—who knows?—
stuffed the carcass nailed on the wall.
Just hide and bone. No elk at all.

CLOCKWORK

Like clockwork that summer
we shared half-an-hour's wedge
of lunchtime sunshine, our faces upturned
and basking in the rays, our sweat sopped sleeves
cooling in the pine-scented breeze. Beside us
an island of trembling wildflowers
huddled around the drain spout,
amidst whistling shards of birdsong
and relentless booms and growls
of railcars coupling and switching nearby.

Paco scooped oranges—for each of us—
from a rust-stained rucksack.
We pushed our thumbs under the rinds,
tore slowly, competing to see who could strip his
in one continuous peel. Hershey bars
we licked from the wrappers in the heat.
And leaned our shoulders against the saw shed,
let our lids fall closed and dream

a ten-minute dream, till the horn
blasted us back to our feet. And we filed
into the incandescent gloom, found our places
inside the machines. As Paco
pulled the switch, the rip-saw screamed,
and lumber hit the green-chain.

As we shoved our earplugs tight, snugged
safety goggles, covered our palms
in leather gloves crusted with pitch,
turned away from each other
and braced our guts for another shift.

INVISIBLE

Last night, snow swathed the meadow.
This morning we scroll the window shades
and trace nature's busy history of trails,
hooves and clawed footfalls crisscrossing
acres blanketed white.

Such complicated comings and goings,
traversing so nearby
while we slumbered unsuspectingly.
Deer, elk, rabbit, squirrel, raccoon,
milling about the moonless overcast midnight.

Even now, invisible birds converse
in the treetops. Beneath winter's crust
an army of voles tunnels and toils
to construct a maze of hidden causeways.
Among beasts, we are bold and obvious and blind.

SUGAR-WHITE BEACHES

Never-ending winter, these months
of snow and ice and gloom. We've lost
long hours again today, pushing back
the leaden blanket of last night's squall,
mounding shoulder-high piles, towering
till they avalanche as if to mock our labors.

The wind whips our cheekbones red
and wet and raw, my wife and I,
our shovels lufting slush, lungs puffing
huffs and grunts . . . when, within a waking dream,
she says, That sugar-white beach
in Isla Mujeres, remember? I nod,

a touch of warmth, a blush, floods over me,
a smile. Side-by-side we replay these memories,
wordlessly, relishing not just the mind's rescue
but something bone-deep having bubbled up
like steaming waters from the earth's core.

DIFFICULT WILD TERRAIN

Cold wind blasting the truck broadside.
Threatening horizons of blue/black
encroaching storms. That image
sticks with me most, the pair of us

bumping along washboard back roads
in search of . . . well, in pursuit of . . .
well, hungry for difficult wild terrain,
sweeping landscapes so unforgivably gorgeous
we'd fallen hushed in reverence and awe.

She recalls we'd stalled mesmerized,
speechless in highland ranch country,
thrilled by an eagle diving through a dervish
of whirling grit, then winging heavenward,
fistful of prairie dog. Finally,

folding himself on a fence rail,
ripping fur and shredding flesh.
The blood, bone and gristle—terrible and revealing—backlit
with roiling torrents of violent sky.
                                                            She and I . . .
a snapshot of a lightning flash
long marriage. I, bedazzled behind the wheel,
and she beside me, reaching to take my hand.

Both of us goose-bumped
in the beauty of hell's wrath, thunder crack,
and cloud bursting downpour. Each of us sheltered
in loving the other. Alive in the world

we were born to explore.

MELISSA KWASNY AND M.L. SMOKER

2019–2021

Near the beginning of our tenure as Montana co-poets laureate, M.L. Smoker and I were invited by the Missoula Art Museum to view their contemporary American Indian art collection—the most extensive in the region—in order to select a work of art and write a poem about it. We chose Lakota artist Molly Murphy Adams' *Epicenter and Impact,* her moving response to the number of missing and murdered indigenous women in Montana. Molly overlaid a vintage Forest Service map of Missoula and the Confederated Salish and Kootenai reservation with beaded red circles and Séliš floral designs to mark where each woman had last gone missing or was assaulted.

The next year, Mandy and I were awarded a fellowship from the Academy of American Poets to spend a year visiting other museums across Montana, writing poems inspired by artwork or objects in their collections, and presenting workshops where students and community members could learn to write their own poems. We envisioned our project not only as a celebration of art and poetry but also as a way of focusing attention on the unique and wonderful museums in our state.

A poem written in response to a work of art is called an *ekphrastic poem.* The term ekphrastic originates from a Greek expression for *description.* In an essay commissioned by Humanities Montana for our project, University of Montana professor Ashby Kinch writes, "The ekphrastic poet models ways of looking at, being with, and responding to, the art work that also model the kinds of curiosity, engagement, and openness that make for a richly lived life."

The poems presented here are based on art and photography from the Missoula Art Museum, the Hockaday Museum of Art, the Museum of the Plains Indian, and the Museum of the Beartooths.

—Melissa Kwasny

Melissa Kwasny is the author of seven books of poetry, including *The Cloud Path, Where Outside the Body is the Soul Today* and *The Nine Senses,* as well as the collection *Earth Recitals: Essays on Image and Vision.* She is also the editor of two anthologies: *I Go to the Ruined Place: Contemporary Poets in Defense of Global Human Rights* and *Toward the Open Field: Poets on the Art of Poetry 1800–1950.* Her recent book of nonfiction, *Putting on the Dog: The Animal Origins of What We Wear,* explores the cultural, labor, and environmental histories of clothing materials provided by animals. Kwasny is the recipient of the Poetry Society of America's Cecil Hemley Award and the Alice Fay Di Castagnola Award and Montana Art Council's Artist's Innovation Award. Kwasny holds an M.F.A. in Poetry and an M.A. in Literature from the University of Montana.

M.L. Smoker is Nakoda, Dakota, and Lakota, an enrolled member of the Fort Peck Tribe. She served as Montana co-poet laureate from 2019–2021 with her friend, Melissa Kwasny. She received an MFA from the University of Montana in Missoula. In 2019 she was recognized as an alumna of the year by the university and received an honorary doctorate in 2023. Her first collection of poems, *Another Attempt at Rescue,* was published by Hanging Loose Press in 2005. She also coauthored both a poetry anthology, *I Go to the Ruined Place: Contemporary Poems in Defense of Global Human Rights* (2019), and a children's graphic novel titled *Thunderous* (2022). She received a regional Emmy award for her work as a writer/consultant on the *PBS* documentary *Indian Relay.*

She served as the director of Indian Education for the State of Montana for ten years, was appointed to the National Advisory Council on Indian Education by President Barack Obama, and currently works at the nonprofit Education Northwest, providing support for Native education efforts around the country.

HEART BUTTE, MONTANA

M. L. Smoker

The unsympathetic wind, how she has evaded me for years now,
leaving a guileless shell and no way to navigate. Once when I stood
on a plateau of earth just at the moment before the dangerous,
jutting peaks converged upon the sway of grasslands, I almost
found a way back. There, the sky, quite possibly all the elements,
caused the rock and soil and vegetation to congregate. Their prayer
was not new and so faint I could hardly discern. Simple remembrances,
like a tiny, syncopated chorus calling everyone home: across
a thousand eastward miles. And what little wind was left at my back.
I could not move and then the music was gone.
All that was left were the springtime faces of mountains, gazing down,
their last patches of snow, luminous. I dreamed of becoming snow melt,
gliding down the slope of history and into the valley. With the promise,
an assurance, that there is always a way to become bird, tree, water again.

BLACK GRIZZLY BEAR ROBE

after a painting by Neil Parsons

Melissa Kwasny

In face-paint, the bear faces you, each eye
tiny, silver, and focused like a star.
Its massive shoulders crowd behind it,
as if waiting for the signal to charge,
but more than mere strength is at play here.
It's a dangerous animal, surely, the first
color you see is blue streaming from its jowls,
leaving trails that dilute, grow dimmer
as they fall, bleeding down its spoiled regalia.
Its forehead is marked with its own totem,
a six-legged theriomorph with horns, splayed
like an inkblot, or a dissected frog,
in consort with eight purple suns around it.
What does it see when it sees you?
A frightened person who hangs her head.
What does it hear? Nervous jingling of bells
before the dance. Smell of white threads
of mycelium. What if you, too, could wear
your spirit, bejeweled with turquoise
and crumpled foil, what if it were the first thing
others see, which has its own shape,
a tree's crown fanning outward. Your hair dyed
a sacred green. Antlers, or perhaps antennae.

THE BOOK OF THE MISSING, MURDERED AND INDIGENOUS– CHAPTER I

For Natalie Smoker

M. L. Smoker

The winding cord of highways, unkempt
gravel roads and the trails of animals –
a record of who and what has passed over,
an agony of secrets.

In the end, they have all borne witness,
eyes like glass beads that can never blink.
The dull light of motel neon shines ominously.
An engine growls across the landscape.

Brittle men who are splintered like glass
thrown from a second story window
and we are the room they leave behind.
They are pathetic husks, feeble in spirit.

Fragments fall along fields and shallow ditches,
in overlooked alleyways or underpasses.
A cold, empty breeze rising from the debris.
The first and last moment of her.

It is rage that pulls her up from this place.
She spews out the wretched and miserable
as particles of dawn-lit soil illuminate her skin.
Her hair is a two-edged sword.

She stitches together the collective story of origin,
her body a map: descended from the stars,
on the backs of animal sisters,
carried to safety in a bird's beak.

BLUE HORSES

are gray, wearing an overcoat of frost,
a swan's wing held against the blue sky.
Roan or dapple, they are a marquee species
amidst the brown herd—the sorrel, bay,
and appaloosa. High on the walls
of the museum rotunda, the buffalo, too,
are circling, among them people, younger
than they will ever be again, their deer
skins soft and carefully beaded. They tell
a story of when snow came in winter,
when rain turned the June meadows green.
Using a technique called *fresco secco,*
sixty years after the buffalo were gone,
thirty million hunted down to a few hundred,
the Blackfeet artist ground dry pigments,
slaked them with lime, bound them
with the plaster forever—just as red ochre
in ancient pictographs became the cliffs.
In the painter's conception of his ancestors,
only one or two generations in the past,
the weather is perfect, plants free of disease.
Picture yourself when you were joyful,
his meditation begins. As if you were
still there. Try to see again through those eyes.

after The Buffalo Hunt *murals by Victor Pepión*

Melissa Kwasny

WE ARE THE ONES

for Dezmond

M. L. Smoker

Waiting.
A syllable: forming,
generating energy in small, dark masses: marrow, stem cell, neuron.
Waiting to come alive again in this tiny body.
Guwa—you should learn this is the word between you and I,
my son, hokshina.
                    Come here. Come home. To this place. Between you and i
no separation. But always room. And silence—until
we can find meaning and the words together.
I repeat it, again and again, gesturing for you to come over. Hoping
the vibrations will come alive, you will listen inside yourself. And you will sense
just who you are, who you belong to and among.
As if you were under water and could feel your pulse,
the whir and swish of your blood traveling miles and miles.
  Across the wind-blown graves of your great grandparents and their grandparents—
Mikushi, Mitugash—yours. And they are out there, belonging to you before
you were even born. Waiting.

MARTIN'S MIDNIGHT FROLIC, 1921

Melissa Kwasny

Who are these people? To whom do they belong?
Scanning the sparse grass, you notice
leather boots and moccasins, the unprepared ground,
stones big enough to trip a running child or horse.

An empty bottle tilts against a white man's feet.
So little joy in their expressions for something
called a frolic. Forty-five years after Custer's defeat
just east of here, then famine, the awful sickening,

the allotments. This rodeo is maybe an uneasy truce.
Cowboy bronc riding, "squaw" relay racing
are on the bill. The Crow have heard about the abuse
at the boarding schools: by 1900, most Native

children were enrolled. It is July Fourth in Absarokee,
Montana, but everyone wears wool blankets
or coats. Some of the men smirk at the camera, wary
of a trick, their bowties tied loosely at their throats.

Three in white aprons and toques blanche: the cooks.
Next to them, two trombones, a snare, a tuba.
A few of the musicians are laughing, as if sharing a joke—
trumpets, clarinets, cornets, a bass drum, and bugles.

It is written that, when they first arrived at the Carlisle
School, each child was given a pointer and told
to pick an English name, though it would be a while
before they learned to read. Of all the names they stole,

which ones survived? A clutch of Indian girls, half-
smiling, in skirts, hold hands under their overlong sleeves.
They lean close like grass stems, wide-eyed as calves,
sly with wonder. They alone seem most ready to believe.

MARK GIBBONS

2021–2023

Richard Hugo, the dean of Montana poetry for my generation, claimed that poetry was a struggle between sound and image, and in the very best poems neither one nor the other dominated. I was reminded of Robert Service's ballads of the Yukon gold rush I fell in love with when I first heard my father read them aloud as a child. I loved the music and the movie his ballads evoked. I grew up on songs, lyrics. Then as I began reading more poetry, I discovered there was a universe of possibilities out there for what a poem could be. It was a verbal expression of an individual trying to connect with others. The only rules for a poem are the rules the poet makes, so new forms are arising constantly. Being a curious and eclectic consumer of poetry and all things, like a kid who had to don a cowboy hat and strap on his gun belt after an episode of *Gunsmoke*, I have tried my hand at almost every poet I've ever read, even the stuff I couldn't comprehend. For me reading and writing poetry are adventures. It's fun to try new things. Of course the penned results of my attempts have my fingerprints all over them. We can't escape our own voice. And that's what I love about all of it, the uniqueness of each poet's voice. It's the same thing I love about each individual I encounter and each morning I open my eyes and still find myself here in this miracle of existence—be it ecstasy or nightmare. For whatever reason, poets are compelled to write and sing about this experience, this paradox of doubt and certainty, this living we chronicle in words. For what it's worth, we believe it's the best we can do.

HUMILITY

I hope I don't die
before I clean out
the basement

There's bound to be
embarrassments down there
for my children

Obviously nothing would
bother me once
I was dead

That said I don't know
why I'd care about
being found out

human by my kids
We all know we are
capable of Shakespearean

faults and vain lusts
blindly murderous impulses
petty jealousies and fooleries

Still it's difficult to let go
of fearful parental roles
patterned after God

that one you thank
out of reflex knowing
you'll be gone

when they discover
you were just another
love-clumsy bag of air

PISSED AT POTTER'S FUNERAL

That frosty November day,
Tom stood at the edge of the grave
we'd dug the night before.
The preacher, stern, Bible in hand,
prayed *God have mercy* on Potter's soul.
Guilty as Potter of too much fun, the rest of us
bowed our heads, bit our tongues,
but Tom never played by the rules.

He whistled, barked out a staccato laugh,
then poured Budweiser on the casket.
His cackle yanked and lashed
every sorry neck erect.
B.W. and Rastus both sprung for him,
grabbed his arms and shook him hard,
hissed he'd better knock it off
or they were going to kick his ass,
but Tom was drunk, beyond, and crazy-strong.
He threatened to piss in the grave.

Only Potter could handle him well,
speaking those low, gentle tones
he'd used to calm horses and dogs.
I watched the pine box in the bottom
of the hole, knew easy was over
for good. Tom struggled to open his zipper.
The three of them almost went down.
Potter's mother let go of the minister's
arm, crossed to Tom and sheltered
his hands with her hands.

She smiled. Her thumbs rubbed
the ridges of his knuckles,
and he melted, bent forward and cried.
She whispered in his ear, slipped her arm
through his arm. The two of them
shuffled away. The wind swayed tall pines
that banked the plot. I looked west,
and two ravens hovered motionless
in currents above the river, then peeled off
and disappeared downstream. There was snow
up Whiskey Gulch. I didn't know what to do,

so I scooped the first shovel of dirt in the grave.
It covered the inlaid cross on the coffin lid
and interred the gifts Tom left
for Potter's journey: a pipe
and beaded medicine pouch—
beside the empty beer can.

LICENSE FOR GHOSTS

we're born with it
the launch code
embedded in our DNA
tiny swastikas
mark that particular spot
the scream hole
that tumbling roll
into our collectively unique
psychoses distraught
the wilderness beyond
our agreed upon delusions
of tree and trout and time
enter truth or death or why
consider fucking
consider the sublime
questioning anything we decide
we must ignore the coffins
the mundane coughing
stop grubbing for whatever
this blind drive to survive
for the most part
keep our eyes on the lies
the stories we tell
of prizes and glories
to avoid our purgatories
these little Heavens in Hell
they say never hand over the keys
never let Chaos drive
if there is a point in being
alive trust the myth-makers
or the scientists
go with the flow
how could we possibly know

more by sleeping with ghosts
we know how to be afraid
to bluff to bully to blame
we know to comfort to love
to try to make it enough
cuz we know enough to know
we don't know enough
the best we can do is huddle
cling to and cuddle each other
gauging this strangeness
this insanely fragile life
we hold so dear
for no clear reason
other than we are here
and yes it is a miracle
and yes I do have a cat
Felix our ninth to be exact
and yes I am married
almost fifty years now
we have two grown sons
survived 24,000-some suns
rising and setting actors
doing this dance of living
here beyond aloof and aware
our self-delusional work
of ignoring the patient elephant
waiting to be recognized
the one Poe loved teasing
amusing muse of mine
and in that regard or toward
that positively brutal end
the only end being yours and mine
the end of this shit shift
I dare you to define it more
precisely or implore me
to lighten and listen up

just pour me a drink instead
and tell your mirror and minions
your virtues and theories
about living this life
maybe retelling the legends again
in the lingo of the flies
about the how and what
of who the fuck we are why
before and after we die
I have tried to crawl inside you
guessing it's what the elephant
wants me to do figuring
there must be a plan
let my ghosts spin it this way
I don't expect you to agree
but I call this poetry my reason
for letting chaos drive

FIRST DATE

for Pam

When I forget that night
at the State Drive-In with you
in the backseat of Christ's
brother's '68 Wildcat,
Elvis ministering to Mary
Tyler Moore's *Change of Habit* . . .
nothing will matter anymore.

When I forget the smells
of your hair and the Wind
Song on your neck, the Coppertoned
skin of your legs & arms against
that tight-white terrycloth
shorts & top outfit, our blood
throbbing, the trickling sweat . . .
nothing of me will remain.

When I can't recollect
the fullness of your mouth
hungering to devour mine,
the anxious embrace of your arms,
your breasts pressing into
my chest, and our tongues
tangoing the ballroom of *yes* . . .
nothing will be left of my mind.

So, today, when you ask me
if I remember this anniversary,
the 43rd since our first date,
I laugh at the silly romance of it all,
duck my head as if someone lurking
overheard—afraid to be found out
a dream lover like you . . .
nothing else has mattered more.

FOR CHRIST'S SAKE

for Colin & Cache

I.

I remember when I was ten
running home again crying
after being held down and whitewashed
by the bully next door. My mother
had heard it too many times before,
pointed me toward the bedroom, "Go
talk to your dad."
                                        Ashamed and afraid,
I didn't move, so she walked me, guiding my shoulders.
Lying in bed, bare chested,
in the dim glow of yellow light, my father
read—a cigarette burning in the ash tray.
He looked at me, then her, put aside his book,
took a drag before butting the smoke.
She left, and I stared at my shoes, tried
to steady shuddery breath.

When he asked, "What's the matter?"
I bawled out the scene, erupted
like a thunderstorm, rained on the floor.
He plucked a couple of tissues from the box
on the headboard, held them out for me,
"Here, you better blow your nose,"
I dabbed and blew, wadded the wet Kleenex.
He took off his glasses, rubbed his chin,
"Aren't you gettin' tired of this?"

"Yes!" I keened.
                                        "Well, what are you going to do?"
"I don't know! He's bigger than me!"
                                                                "Yeah, that's true,

but he won't stop until you make him.
Just one good lick is all it takes,
and he'll think twice about picking on you."
                                                            I nodded,
grinned, blinked away tears. My father winked,
"Good night," and I knew it was.

Back in bed, I rehearsed my death,
relished the bloody surprise:
my answering fists slashing,
lashing out at the panicked clown hiding in the bully's eyes.

II.

I am working in Shelby, Montana,
when Littleton, Colorado, goes down;
watch it played out on the TV news
alone in my motel room—the blood bath viewed
on "security" tapes.
                                    When I call home,
my son answers the phone. It's good
to hear his voice, to know I needn't worry,
imagine the worst—burying him today.
                                                       He tells me
some kid got beat up in the park
across from his school for calling this "hick"
a "fag". He swears these homophobic
bullies brag about hating queers,
says they beat up a girl on the street
last week because she's a lesbian.

My son is ready to "kill the bastards"
(and I want to help him kick some ass).
                                                       On TV
SWAT teams are "still finding bodies,"
rifling through Columbine.

"Somebody needs to call the principal,
the police, or their goddamn parents," I insist.
My son doesn't believe the cops can help.

I try to convince him, myself,
we're evolving, becoming kinder . . .
yet we keep on killing Cain
in the name of Christ. For the love of Jesus,
does it make sense to you? Peace.
Forgiveness, turn your cheek. Lay down
your life for love. The Trench Coat Mafia
bleeds on the stairs, the cafeteria floor.

I tell my son to let it go.
                                        I don't know
what a coward is. I do know
a cornered animal is dangerous—
I've been there, ready to kill. There's nothing
more volatile than the smoldering fire
inside a humiliated man.

CHRIS LA TRAY

2023–2025

Eleventh Montana poet laureate Chris La Tray approaches the practice of poetry the same as he does the spiritual life of an Anishinaabe person: which is to say, if one lives an Anishinaabe life, with particular attention to the seven guiding principles of the Seven Grandfather teachings—Humility, Courage, Honesty, Wisdom, Truth, Respect, and Love—then every footstep becomes a prayer. If one approaches poetry in a similar fashion, recognizing that everything that happens may be viewed as a poem, and that every moment in life is an experience best paid constant and careful attention to, then every footstep becomes a poem. Whether as words on a page or shared orally, poetry becomes another means for telling and sharing stories; La Tray's work as a poet and storyteller exists to remind people that their stories matter, that they are the only ones who can properly tell them, and that poetry, however it is defined, is a beautiful means for doing so.

Chris La Tray is a Métis storyteller, a descendent of the Pembina Band of the mighty Red River of the North and an enrolled member of the Little Shell Tribe of Chippewa Indians. His third book, *Becoming Little Shell: A Landless Indian's Journey Home,* a memoir, was published by Milkweed Editions on August 20, 2024. His first book, *One-Sentence Journal: Short Poems and Essays from the World at Large,* won the 2018 Montana Book Award and a 2019 High Plains Book Award. His book of haiku and haibun poetry, *Descended from a Travel-worn Satchel,* was published in 2021 by Foothills Publishing. Chris writes the weekly newsletter "An Irritable Métis" and lives near Frenchtown, Montana.

COMET

Blaze through your meager time on earth like a gigantic rock firing through space at an unimaginable distance from where you slide behind the wheel of an iron-plated old Chevrolet, gravel tail arcing behind you as your tires, attached to rims, attached to axle, attached to drive train, attached to a few decades of classic Detroit engineering blast you away from all of your pain and frustration like a rocket into an entirely different universe of troubles, the kinetic energy of all those horses under the hood vibrating the flesh of your legs and your belly and you can't help but grin in spite of every little thing you perceive as wrong with your world, not sure where you're headed but you'll know when you get there, even if it's a crash of impact and a whomp! of fireball that sends your final prayers into the sky as tiny little fortunes scrawled on pieces of smoldering ash.

HOLY

after the quote, "The poet is the priest of the invisible," from Wallace Stevens

If a poet is a priest then I guess
it is time to quit writing poems,
because I don't aspire to be the leader,
spiritual or otherwise, of anything.

To say nothing of the baggage that
comes attached to such a word,
like a bloated and infected tick
spreading sickness and slow, painful death.

Tell me where any priest has ever gone
where the souls already there
are any better off for it?

I prefer my poems, like my spirit,
to lean more heathen,
away from any notion of
robe-wearing devils
preaching salvation from behind
the muzzles of colonial rifles
disguised as scripture.

Justify the missionary's existence
all you want.
But first acknowledge their invisible,
those unmarked graves
left in their wake.

Of course it was some high-minded,
self-important aristocrat
who sought to sanctify
his literary efforts,
but c'mon.

These poems are words.
A spell, certainly for some.
A refuge even, for others.

But my people have no use for
the ivory towers and glossy pages
that vomit forth that brand
of pretentious self-reference.

Go forage for roots on prairie ploughed over.
Spend a couple days fruitlessly looking for meat
where once it was abundant.
Watch all of your efforts wither under
the onslaught of a relentless sun.
Tell me then what is holy.

40 DEGREE PLUNGE

Curtains open to charcoal light at 7 a.m.
and juncos cling to frozen branches.

The rear tires of a hooptie churn and slide
through smooth drifts collecting

at the hard-right corner of the street,
snow still falling on my neighborhood.

In the kitty-corner driveway
a hulking black Chevy rumbles,

billowing clouds of hot exhaust swept away
on the gusts of wind that doubles-over

the ponderosa and blasts snow sidewise
first in one direction, then the next.

I go outside with wet hair under my cap
and my beard freezes crispy.

Two rabbits huddled under my front porch
don't so much as shudder as I pass.

I wonder about the young woman next door
with the five kids and two broken cars.

Is she still in tears for the man
cuffed and shoved, yesterday afternoon,

into the back of a deputy's cruiser,
one of three in the street before our homes,

parked so they blocked all of us in,
when the air was still and the temperature

was at least 40 degrees warmer?
We won't thaw out all week.

ABOUT THE MONTANA POET LAUREATE

"Genuine poetry can communicate before it is understood."
T. S. Eliot

Poetry is powerful because it is one of the most primitive forms of public art. The recitation of language using cadence, rhythm, and the mnemonic device of rhyme has been around since the beginning of human time. Its power lies so deep within us that just listening to poetry can calm anxiety, boost moods, and elevate emotional well-being.

The Montana State Legislature created the position of Montana poet laureate in 2005 with the goal of advancing and supporting the poetic arts. The poet laureate's task is to reach out to communities across Montana to promote the appreciation of poetry as an ancient and ongoing form of expression.

It is an honorary post—unpaid, by current statute—though any former poet laureate could tell you what an enormous burden the honor places on the poets. (The Montana Arts Council does reimburse travel costs, and there are some speaker honoraria supported by Humanities Montana.) Poets laureate each serve a term of two years. Nomination to the position is available to poets residing in Montana whose work exhibits artistic excellence and achievement, ongoing contributions to the cultural community, and worthiness of statewide recognition. Any Montanan may nominate a poet for the post by contacting the Montana Arts Council.

A panel drawn from members of the literary community select finalists from among the nominations, and they submit these finalists to the Montana Arts Council board for review and approval. The Arts Council then submits three nominees to the governor, who selects the poet laureate for the upcoming biennium. To date, eleven poets laureate have served in ten two-year terms.

PUBLICATION HISTORY

"Begin Again," "Mothers," and "Imago" by permission of Sandra Alcosser.

"Tracks & Traces," "The Wooly Mammoths," and "The Spell Of The Bitterroot" appear in *Four Swans,* Lynx House Press, 2013, by permission.

"Odd Numbered Geese," "Rivers Of Horse," "Earth Day," and "Mass In Crow" appear in *Horse Tracks,* Lost Horse Press, 2020, by permission.

"In Your Sleep," "Whore," and "Ides Of March" appear by permission of Lost Horse Press, 2020.

"She Was So Tiny" and "Deer On Crazy Creek" appear in *What Does Not Return,* Lost Horse Press, 2018, by permission.

"A Colander Of Barley" appear in *When We Wake In the Night,* Word Tech Editions, 2012, by permission.

"The Train" and "Preparing To Paint The Body Of The Dead Christ In the Tomb" appear in *Iggy Horse,* Wave Books, 2023, by permission.

"He Quickly Told His Life Story" appears in *Thin Kimono,* Wave Books, 2010, by permission.

"Elk" appears in *The Owen Wister Review, Atlanta Review;* originally published in *Or Maybe I Drift Off Alone*, Shabda Press, 2016, by permission.

"Clockwork" appears in *Atlanta Review;* originally published in *Or Maybe I Drift Off Alone,* Shabda Press 2016, by permission.

"Invisible" appears in *Hawaii Pacific Review, Big Sky Journal*; originally published in *Earth-blood & Star-shine,* Shabda Press, 2018, by permission.

"Sugar-White Beaches" appears in *Burningword Literary Journal, Ice Fishing with Fourth Graders,* Shabda Press, 2020, by permission.

"Difficult Wild Terrain" appears in *Goodness* (Anthology). Wising Up Press, 2020; *Ice Fishing with Fourth Graders,* Shabda Press, 2020, by permission.

"Black Grizzly Bear Robe," "Blue Horses," and "Martin's Midnight Frolic, 1921" appear in *Ekphrastic Poetry* on humanitiesmontana.org, by permission.

"Heart Butte, Montana" appears in *New Poets of Native Nations,* Graywolf Press, 2018, by permission.

"The Book Of The Missing, Murdered And Indigenous– Chapter 1" appears in *Living Nations, Living Words,* AFC 2020/004, American Folklife Center, Library of Congress, by permission.

"We Are The Ones" appears in *Back Forty*, *Big Sky Journal,* 2016, by permission.

"Humility" and "License For Ghosts" appear in *In the Weeds,* Drumlummon Institute, 2021, by permission.

"Pissed At Potter's Funeral" appears in *Connemara Moonshine,* Camphorweed Press, 2002, by permission.

"First Date" appears in *mostly cloudy,* FootHills Publishing, 2020, by permission.

"For Christ's Sake" appears in *blue horizon,* Two Dogs Press, 2007, by permission.

"Comet," "Holy," and "40 Degree Plunge" are first published in this anthology.

Jim Harrison, excerpt from "Solstice Litany" from *Dead Man's Float.* Copyright © 2016 by Jim Harrison. Reprinted with the permission of The Permissions Company, LLC, on behalf of Copper Canyon Press, coppercanyonpress.org.

ABOUT THE MONTANA ARTS COUNCIL

The Montana Arts Council is the agency of state government established to develop the creative potential of all Montanans, advance education, spur economic vibrancy, and revitalize communities through involvement in the arts. Founded in 1965 and funded by the State of Montana and the National Endowment for the Arts, the Montana Arts Council works to bring the creative power of art to every corner of Big Sky Country to invigorate the cultural, economic, and social heritage of all who live and work in the Last Best Place.

ABOUT THE MONTANA HISTORICAL SOCIETY

The Montana Historical Society (MTHS) is the guardian of Montana's memory. Established in 1865—one of the oldest institutions of its kind in the West—the MTHS's vast historic collections of artifacts, photographs, and documents are exhibited in six extraordinary galleries. In 1969, MTHS became the official state archives and the repository for state agency records of permanent value.

Since the founding of the Montana Historical Society in Bannack in 1865, its historians, curators, and educators have worked as a team to save and share the stories of Montana.

The mission of the Montana Historical Society is to save Montana's past, share our stories, and inspire exploration, to provide meaning for today and vision for tomorrow.

A NOTE ON THE TYPE

This book is set in Mantinia, designed by Matthew Carter, and Minion, designed by Robert Slimbach. Mantinia and Minion are released by Carter & Cone Type and Adobe, respectively.